Puffy really
Love's to play
ball.

Puffy starts
hitting the ball.

When Puffy hits
the ball he gets
Pricked.
Puffy says Ouch!

Puffy grabs the ball again and he realizes it is his friend little Puffy.

little Puffy says ouch, why are you hitting me?

Puffy says "I am Sorry" I didn't realize it was you.

little Puffy says
what?
How do you not
realize when we
look exactly the
same?

Puffy says the reflection of the water moving tricked my perception.

little Puffy says,
oh I see, well if you
look closely you can
see I am not a ball.

Puffy says you are
correct and I am
sorry.

Puffy and little Puffy
hugged and swam
of together.

Puffy and little Puffy learned?

A.) They are both angry

B.) They can hit each other

C.) They had different Perceptions

Puffy and little Puffy used what skills?

A.) Playing ball
B.) Anger
C.) Hitting
D.) Communication

1.) Puffy and little Puffy
   realized "B" "They are friends".

2.) Puffy and little Puffy
   learned "C" "They had
   different perceptions.

3.) Puffy and little Puffy
   used "D" communication
   skills.

1) Puffy and little Puffy realized "B" "They are friends".

2.) Puffy and little Puffy learned "C" "They had different perceptions.

3.) Puffy and little Puffy used "D" communication skills.

Contribution by
Matthew J. Thorn

color me

color me

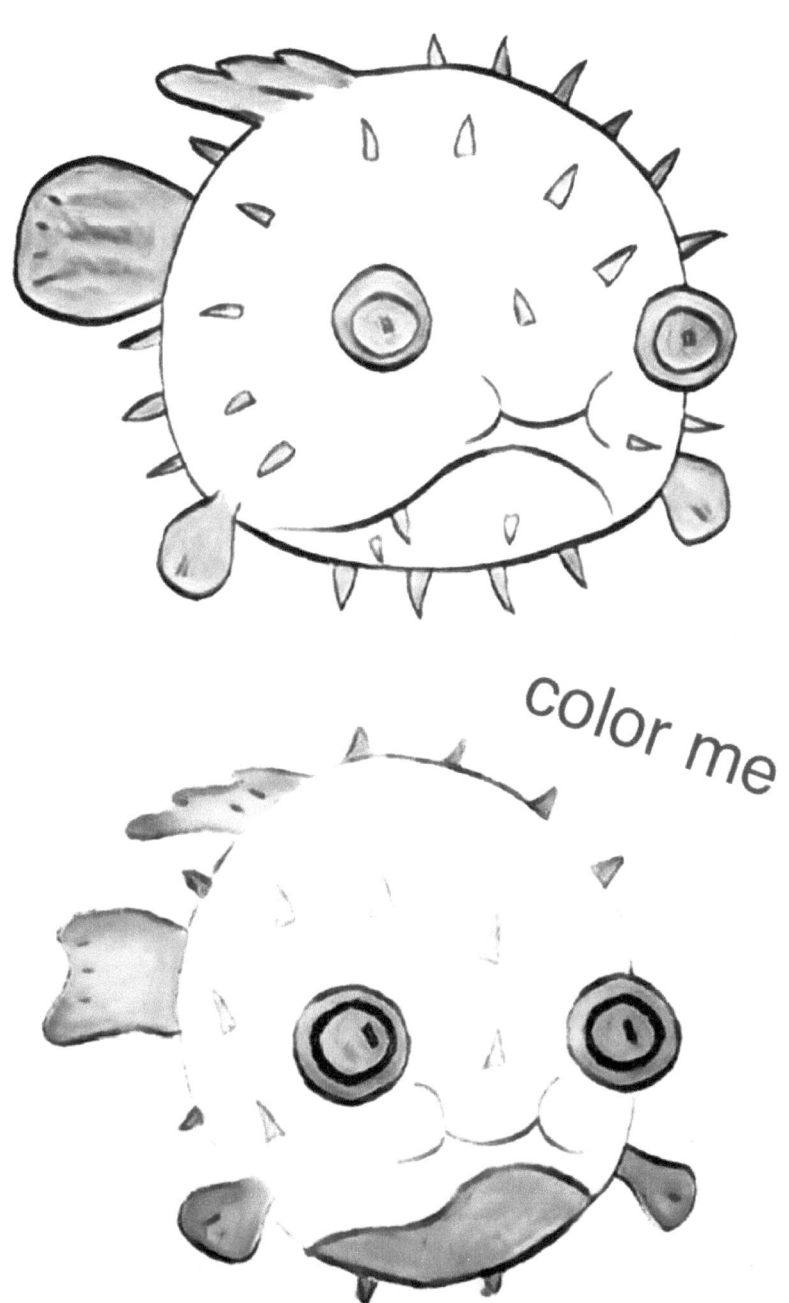

color me

www.ingramcontent.com/pod-product-compliance
Lightning Source LLC
Chambersburg PA
CBHW050908290526
45792CB00002B/748